Lasting
Lines

100 poems and
poets that
you should know

Jamie Grant

hardie grant books

Contents

Introduction

The English language is rich in poetry. We often hear this phrase used to describe the depths and quirkiness of English words and idioms, but it is also a purely literal observation. Many of the catch phrases, familiar expressions and truisms that we use unthinkingly, whether in conversation or in written communication, have their origin in lines of poetry. There are so many such lines, in fact, that it might not be possible to compile a truly exhaustive list of them. There is a much-repeated joke about the reader new to Shakespeare who complained that the plays were full of clichés.

The idea of this collection is to assemble a selection of those lines from the poetry published in English from the earliest days of the printing press to the present. Beyond the limiting template of a single poem per poet, up to the magical number of one hundred, the only organising principle has been the taste, and interests, of the selector – anybody else might have undertaken a similar selection without choosing a single line in common. Anybody else, indeed, might profit from attempting such an exercise.

When it was first suggested to me that I should compile this collection, I felt it might be an arduous task. Instead, it has been an undertaking of sheer delight. There were many lines that had been lodged in my memory ever since my first reading of them, but it seemed best to return to the context in which each reading had been made, and thus to re-read all of the poets I had long admired. The delight lay in the re-reading, and thus it is my suggestion that every reader should assemble a comparable selection of their own favourite lines and enjoy the process just as much as I have.

While particular lines are the focus of the collection, it is to be hoped that each excerpt will encourage a return to the poem it has been extracted from, and in turn to the other works of the poem's author. Some lines will be familiar to everyone, and others unexpected; as the choices come nearer to the present, there may be lines that are not yet part of our language but may become so in the future.

In reading the various poets in chronological order over the centuries, it has been instructive for me to note how styles, techniques and subjects have evolved; thus, almost by accident, this collection amounts to a highly abbreviated history of the development of English-language poetry. That history includes geography, as it reflects how poetry written in English began to emerge in the far-flung settings of Britain's former colonies.

The politics and economics of the poetry-writing profession are also included. In researching the lives of the poets for the brief notes attached to my selections, I was struck by the variety of occupations and social positions poets have held over the centuries (in the twentieth century most of them seem to have been university teachers, while in the sixteenth century they were usually government officials or clergymen), and struck, too, by how many of the best-loved poets in the language did not publish their work in their own lifetime. I also could not have failed to notice how the lives of poets have often been intertwined with those of other poets.

Thus, anyone who reads this collection from beginning to end will find that narrative threads extend from one life to another, while certain themes echo from one line to the next. These themes include monarchy and republicanism, America and Australia, what Shakespeare refers to as 'country matters', poet laureates, the Nobel Prize for Literature, sport, war, death and Bob Dylan. There is no obligation to read it in this way, however. As with every anthology, it is possible for the reader to dip in and out, like a duck feeding in a pond, and return to the surface with at least some feeling of nourishment.

Chaucer, who worked as a tax collector and a Member of Parliament, was the first Englishman to write serious poetry in his contemporary vernacular — a form of Middle English — rather than in French or Latin. As the opening of his major poem *The Canterbury Tales* suggests, he also was the first poet to mention climate change.

Whan that April with his showres soote

The droughte of March hath perced to the roote

FROM *THE CANTERBURY TALES*, BY

Geoffrey Chaucer

(1343–1400)

These lines from a much-recited traditional ballad were to reappear, unacknowledged, in the work of a modern balladist, Bob Dylan, in his song 'A Hard Rain'. This and other quotations so impressed the Swedish judges that they awarded the Nobel Prize for Literature to the American popular singer-songwriter, the first time a prize for literature had been awarded to a musician. So far no poet has been given a prize for music.

'O where ha' you been, Lord Randal, my son?
And where ha' you been, my handsome young man?'
'I ha' been at the greenwood, mother, mak my bed soon,
For I'm wearied wi' huntin', and fain wad lie down.'

FROM 'LORD RANDAL',

Anonymous ballad

(FIFTEENTH OR SIXTEENTH CENTURY)

Before she became queen, Elizabeth Tudor was educated in the ways expected of female aristocrats of her time, acquiring skills as a linguist and writer among other accomplishments. The death of her half-sister Mary led to her accession to the throne at the age of twenty-five. While many attempts were made to arrange her marriage to various foreign monarchs, she remained what she promoted herself as: the 'Virgin Queen'. This poem was her explanation of her unmarried condition; it was one of a number of poems she wrote, though none were published in her lifetime. In a speech she declared, 'I know that I have the body of a weak and feeble woman, but I have the heart and stomach of a king'.

When I was fair and young, then favor graced me.

Of many was I sought their mistress for to be.

But I did scorn them all and answered them therefore:

Go, go, go, seek some other where, importune me

no more.

FROM 'WHEN I WAS FAIR AND YOUNG', BY

Queen Elizabeth I

(1533–1603)

Australian Prime Minister Sir Robert Menzies quoted these lines in front of the visiting Queen Elizabeth II not long after her coronation, and was widely condemned for doing so. Republicans felt it to be excessively deferential towards the monarchy, while other critics, not recognising the quotation, suspected him of making up the lines himself and hence of being guilty of bad poetry. Others found it inappropriate for the stout, dense-eyebrowed, white-haired politician to be speaking in such terms to the young, attractive queen.

There is a lady sweet and kind,
Was never face so pleased my mind;
I did but see her passing by,
And yet I love her till I die.

FROM 'THERE IS A LADY SWEET AND KIND',

Anonymous ballad

(FIRST COLLECTED IN 1607)

Shakespeare was a professional actor who was called upon to deliver playscripts for his troupe to perform. Drawing on pre-existing stories, and on the facts set out in *Holinshed's Chronicles*, a contemporary history of Britain, he became inadvertently the greatest writer in the English language. This was not the result of the plots he devised, or the characters he created, but rather his rich, inventive and profound use of language. This made him the most quotable (and quoted) writer in English literature. So many phrases from his plays and poems have entered our language permanently that it is difficult to find a passage in his works that seems unfamiliar. As they are all written in the form of blank verse, his plays are considered to be poems as much as his sonnets and the other poetic narratives he produced in the years when London's theatres were closed due to an outbreak of bubonic plague. As the fragments of dialogue quoted here show, he also displayed an appetite for bawdy word play, or, as a Victorian era editor put it, 'I suspect some indelicate suggestion.' I have made an exception to this collection's rule that each author should supply a single quotation, as Shakespeare's works are so rich that a quotable line can be found in any of his plays by opening a page at random. Instead, I have limited my quotations to a single play, arguably Shakespeare's best, though it could equally be argued that *King Lear, Macbeth, Othello* or *The Merchant of Venice* deserves that distinction.

Polonius. Neither a borrower nor a lender be;

For loan oft loses both itself and friend,

And borrowing dulls the edge of husbandry.

* * *

Horatio. O day and night, but this is wondrous strange!

Hamlet. And therefore as a stranger give it welcome.

There are more things in heaven and earth, Horatio,

Than are dreamt of in your philosophy.

* * *

Hamlet. Lady, shall I lie in your lap?

Ophelia. No, my lord.

Hamlet. I mean, my head upon your lap?

Ophelia. Ay, my lord.

Hamlet. Do you think I meant country matters?

Ophelia. I think nothing, my lord.

Hamlet. That's a fair thought to lie between maid's legs.

FROM *HAMLET*, BY

William Shakespeare

(1564–1616)

Jonson lived a colourful life, working as a bricklayer and volunteering for military service in the Low Countries before becoming an actor and playwright. In 1598, he narrowly escaped hanging after he killed another actor in a duel. In the same year he converted to Catholicism; he was subsequently charged with 'popery' and treason, but eventually found favour with King James I and was awarded a generous pension. As a contemporary of Shakespeare, he knew his fellow actor and playwright well, and, unlike the eccentric conspiracy theorists from the nineteenth century onwards, saw no reason to query the authorship of Shakespeare's works. Jonson contributed a poem entitled 'To the Memory of My Beloved, the Author Mr William Shakespeare' to the first published edition of the plays.

Drink to me only with thine eyes,

And I will pledge with mine;

Or leave a kiss but in the cup,

And I'll not look for wine.

FROM 'SONG: TO CELIA', BY

Ben Jonson

(1572–1637)

The sun personified as a foolish old busy-body, like Polonius in Shakespeare's *Hamlet*, interrupting the poet's sleep-in, appeals to many readers. John Donne lived an adventurous early life, travelling widely, joining a naval expedition against Spain and marrying twice, before he took holy orders in the Church of England and became the Dean of St Paul's Cathedral in London, where his sermons were celebrated and highly popular and his marble effigy can still be seen. Only his prose writings were published in his lifetime, but even as a young man he was described by a contemporary as 'not dissolute but very neat, a great visitor of ladies, a great frequenter of plays, a great writer of conceited verses'.

Busy old fool, unruly sun,

Why dost thou thus,

Through windows, and through curtains call on us?

FROM 'THE SUN RISING', BY

John Donne

(1572–1631)

Like Donne, Herrick was a clergyman with a taste for the erotic and the sensual; in his poem addressed 'To the Virgins' he advised 'Gather ye rosebuds while ye may', and his poem 'Upon Julia's Breasts' concludes 'Between whose glories, there my lips I'll lay, / Ravished in that fair Via Lactea'. Educated at Cambridge, he was a friend of Ben Jonson, and his prolific poetic output was popular in London, even though he lived in distant Devon. In 1647 he was deprived of his clergyman's living by the republican government because he remained a Royalist; he resumed his living after the Restoration of 1660.

A sweet disorder in the dress

Kindles in clothes a wantonness.

FROM 'DELIGHT IN DISORDER', BY

Robert Herrick

(1591–1674)

A gifted Greek and Latin scholar also fluent in Spanish, Italian and French, an accomplished musician and a Cambridge University academic, George Herbert seemed destined for high political office when he became a Member of Parliament and began to enjoy the patronage of King James I. Instead, the death of the king led him to resign from parliament and take holy orders, following which he became Rector of Bemerton, an obscure rural parish, in 1630. Like his older brother Edward, otherwise known as Lord Herbert of Cherbury, he wrote poetry for most of his life, but he made no effort to publish it until he knew his death from consumption was approaching. He then sent a copy of his book *The Temple* to Nicholas Ferrar, the founder of a utopian religious community at Little Gidding in Cambridgeshire, who also happened to be a bookbinder. Herbert asked Ferrar to burn his book or print it, as he saw fit.

Sweet day, so cool, so calm, so bright,

The bridal of the earth and sky:

The dew shall weep thy fall tonight;

                 For thou must die.

FROM 'VIRTUE', BY

George Herbert

(1593–1633)

Educated at Christ's College, Cambridge, Milton wrote some of his early poems in Latin; as a result, he was received with distinction in the Italian academic world when he travelled abroad in the late 1630s; in the course of this tour he came to meet with Galileo. He returned to England in order to take part in the Civil War on the side of the Parliamentarians, and after the execution of King Charles I he was appointed Latin secretary to Cromwell and became an official apologist for the Commonwealth, as the republican regime was known. After the Restoration he went into hiding, and only then did he complete some of his major works, including 'Paradise Lost' and 'Samson Agonistes'. He had gone blind in 1652, but this had no effect on his mastery of English syntax; he also married three times and was an early advocate for the practice of divorce.

O how unlike
To that first naked glory! Such of late
Columbus found th' American, so girt
With feathered cincture, naked else and wild
Among the trees on isles and woody shores.

FROM 'PARADISE LOST', BY

John Milton

(1608–1674)

Born in England, Anne Bradstreet migrated to America in her late teens with her husband Simon Bradstreet, who was to become governor of the Massachusetts Bay Colony. She managed to write poetry even while raising eight children. When her book *The Tenth Muse Lately Sprung Up in America* was published by her brother-in-law, it was without her knowledge, as the extract opposite recounts. She is considered to be the first American poet, and inspired John Berryman's poem 'Homage to Mistress Bradstreet'.

Thou ill-formed offspring of my feeble brain,

Who after birth didst by my side remain,

Till snatched from thence by friends, less wise than true,

Who thee abroad, exposed to public view

FROM 'THE AUTHOR TO HER BOOK', BY

Anne Bradstreet

(1612–1672)

Andrew Marvell grew up in Hull, the provincial city known centuries later as the home of Philip Larkin, and, after receiving his degree from Trinity College, Cambridge, travelled widely in Europe. He became tutor to the daughter of Lord Fairfax, who had been the supreme commander of the Parliamentarian army at the battle of Naseby, after which King Charles I was overthrown and the British monarchy replaced by a republic. Marvell then became tutor to a ward of Oliver Cromwell, who was the head of the new Parliamentarian government under the title of Lord Protector, before being appointed assistant to the poet John Milton, secretary to the republican Council of State. Marvell was elected as a Member of Parliament in 1659, after the death of Cromwell but before the monarchy had been restored, and he remained the MP for Hull for the rest of his life. 'To His Coy Mistress' may be the most famous of his poems, but he also wrote about the gardens on the Fairfax country estate, and 'An Horatian Ode Upon Cromwell's Return from Ireland'.

The grave's a fine and private place,

But none, I think, do there embrace.

FROM 'TO HIS COY MISTRESS', BY

Andrew Marvell

(1621–1678)

Rochester's much-quoted comment on Charles II was somewhat unkind, given that the king had awarded him a pension when he was just fourteen years old and had forgiven him repeatedly for such misdeeds as the abduction of an heiress, the murder of a constable, an insulting remark about the king's mistress, and the mistake of giving the king a copy of a bawdy poem that satirised him ('Poor prince! Thy prick, like thy buffoons at Court / Will govern thee, because it makes thee sport.'). Despite these escapades, and others like them, Rochester was made a Gentleman of the Bedchamber in 1666, a captain in the Horse Guards in 1667, Gamekeeper for the County of Oxford in 1668, and Deputy Lieutenant of Somerset in 1672. At the same time he was leading such a debauched life that he claimed to have been continually drunk for five years. At the end of his short life, he converted to Christianity.

God bless our good and gracious King,

   Whose promise none relies on;

Who never said a foolish thing,

   Nor ever did a wise one.

'EPIGRAM ON CHARLES II', BY

John Wilmot, Earl of Rochester

(1647–1680)

In Swift's poem, Strephon (like Celia, a conventional figure in the pastoral poetry of the time) steals into the room where Celia has spent five hours in dressing, only to be horrified by the discovery of a bedpan in her cabinet. Born in Ireland, Swift was, like Donne and Herrick, a clergyman who nonetheless wrote candidly about bodily details and secular reality. He had been involved in politics before he accepted the position of Dean of St Patrick's Cathedral in Dublin, which he saw as 'exile' from a life in London, where he had moved in literary and political circles. In Dublin, Swift wrote the satirical *Gulliver's Travels*, the book for which he is now best known.

Thus finishing his grand survey,

Disgusted Strephon stole away

Repeating in his amorous fits,

Oh! Celia, Celia, Celia shits!

FROM 'THE LADY'S DRESSING ROOM', BY

Jonathan Swift

(1667–1745)

Born into a Catholic family at the time of the Glorious Revolution, Pope was not allowed to attend university due to his religion, and was instead largely self-educated. At the age of twelve he suffered a childhood illness that stunted his growth. From early on he was a prolific writer, producing an 'Ode to Solitude' in the year of his illness, and he was still in his twenties when 'An Essay on Criticism' and 'The Rape of the Lock' established his reputation. Though to some readers the heroic couplets he used in much of his work seem monotonous, his poems are full of memorable phrases that have entered the language. In the 1960s the conviction of Mick Jagger on drug charges inspired an editorial in *The Times* quoting Pope: 'Who breaks a butterfly upon a wheel?' The success of Pope's translation of the *Iliad* was such that he was able to buy a large house at Twickenham, a part of London better known now for its rugby stadium.

View him with scornful, yet with jealous eyes,

And for arts that caused himself to rise,

Damn with faint praise, assent with civil leer,

And without sneering, teach the rest to sneer;

FROM 'EPISTLE TO DR ARBUTHNOT', BY

Alexander Pope

(1688-1744)

Almost a century after the republican experiment had failed, English poets still drew on it as a source of imagery and subject matter. Thomas Gray expected his readers to be familiar with Cromwell's bloodthirsty regime, and in the only poem he is famous for he expressed, according to Dr Johnson, 'sentiments to which every bosom returns an echo'. Gray lived a quiet academic life and was not a prolific poet, but he did write an 'Ode On the Death of a Favourite Cat, Drowned in a Tub of Goldfishes'. Christopher Smart is reported to have said, 'Thomas Gray walks as if he had fouled his small-clothes and looks as if he smelt it'.

Some mute inglorious Milton here may rest,

Some Cromwell guiltless of his country's blood.

FROM 'ELEGY WRITTEN IN A COUNTRY
CHURCHYARD', BY

Thomas Gray

(1716–1771)

Christopher Smart was a brilliant classical scholar at Cambridge University, but in his twenties he began to show signs of what we would now see as obsessive-compulsive disorder (including a compulsion to pray in public), but was then regarded simply as madness. He was committed to the lunatics' ward at St Luke's Hospital, along with his cat, and wrote his best-known poem while confined there. Though he was later released from hospital, he ended his days in a debtors' prison.

For I will consider my Cat Jeoffry.

For he is the servant of the Living God, duly and daily serving him.

For at the first glance of the glory of God in the East he worships in his way.

For this is done by wreathing his body seven times round with elegant quickness.

FROM 'JUBILATE AGNO', BY

Christopher Smart

(1722–1771)

The battle on Flodden Field took place in 1513, but Elliot's poem commemorating the battle was first published in 1756. Her lament was admired by Robert Burns and by Walter Scott, who approved its imitation of the 'manner of the ancient minstrels'. Elliot was born in Teviotdale in Scotland; her nephew, the Reverend Robert Elliot, was also an aspiring poet, who sent his work to Scott in the hope of similar approval. His daughter, Eleanor, married Dr James Grant of Jedburgh before migrating to Australia.

I've heard them lilting at the ewe-milking,

　Lasses a' lilting before dawn of day;

But now they are moaning on ilka green loaning –

　The Flowers of the Forest are a' wede away.

FROM 'LAMENT FOR FLODDEN', BY

Jean Elliot

(1727–1805)

Cowper studied law, and was called to the Bar, but never practised, as his chronic depression declined into madness and led to an attempted suicide. He was treated in an asylum, where he found consolation in evangelical Christianity. As was the case with his near-contemporary Christopher Smart, religion and insanity seemed to go hand in hand. Though Cowper is no longer regarded as a major poet, it is surprising how many phrases from his poems have entered the language as stock expressions, such as the ones opposite or the opening line of his poem 'The Solitude of Alexander Selkirk', 'I am monarch of all I survey'.

God moves in a mysterious way,

His wonders to perform;

He plants his footsteps in the sea,

And rides upon the storm.

FROM 'OLNEY HYMNS', BY

William Cowper

(1731–1800)

n the 1960s, believers in 'alternate lifestyles' were greatly inspired by the words of William Blake, taking the first of the proverbs quoted above as their guiding principle. Posters of Blake's poems and engravings were displayed on the walls of many a communal house or squat. Yet the poet's intentions had been taken out of context; as the title of his series of proverbs is meant to indicate, these ideas were the reverse of his true beliefs. Blake was apprenticed as an engraver at an early age, and was largely self-educated; he printed and published his own books, but met with little success in his life-time. Yet he is recognised now as one of the great geniuses of his age, both as poet and artist, even though many of his visionary notions verge on the madness that afflicted Cowper and Smart.

The road of excess leads to the palace of wisdom.

* * *

If the fool would persist in his folly he would
  become wise.

* * *

The nakedness of women is the work of God.

* * *

What is now proved was once only imagin'd.

FROM 'PROVERBS OF HELL', BY

William Blake

(1757–1827)

Robert Burns remains one of the most popular, and widely quoted and recited, poets in the world. His statue can be seen in city parks wherever there are annual Burns Nights and Burns Societies, which includes all of the countries where Scottish immigrants settled in the eighteenth and nineteenth centuries, while his poem 'Auld Lang Syne' is sung at New Year's Eve celebrations almost everywhere. His popularity among English-language readers has in no way suffered from the fact that his poems were not written in English but a version of Scots dialect; an inability to understand them is no barrier to enjoyment. Burns used standard English when he needed to, as when writing letters in his capacity as an excise officer towards the end of his short life. It was a life packed with incident, of which he could write, 'The sweetest hours that e'er I spend, / Are spent among the lasses, O'. By the end of his life he had fathered at least thirteen children by at least five different women.

O wad some Pow'r the giftie gie us

To see oursels as ithers see us!

It wad frae monie a blunder free us,

    An' foolish notion:

What airs in dress an' gait wad lea'e us,

    An' ev'n devotion!

FROM 'TO A LOUSE', BY

Robert Burns

(1759–1796)

Wordsworth was orphaned at an early age, and was sent to board in England's Lake District before he completed his education at Trinity College, Cambridge. He travelled in France and Switzerland soon after the French Revolution, and fathered an illegitimate child while he was abroad. On his return to England he met Samuel Taylor Coleridge, with whom he published *Lyrical Ballads* in 1798 – this revolutionary collection opens with Coleridge's 'Rime of the Ancient Mariner' and closes with 'Tintern Abbey'. For the book's second edition Wordsworth wrote a preface that explained the principles behind his writing, including his ideas that the poet's voice should be that of 'a man speaking to men' and that poetry should be 'strong emotion recollected in tranquility'. For a time Wordsworth and his sister, Dorothy, lived with Coleridge in Somerset, but then they moved to Grasmere in the Lake District, where they remained for the rest of their lives. In 1843 Wordsworth was appointed Poet Laureate by Queen Victoria.

I have learned
To look on nature, not as in the hour
Of thoughtless youth; but hearing oftentimes
The still, sad music of humanity

FROM 'LINES COMPOSED A FEW MILES
ABOVE TINTERN ABBEY', BY

William Wordsworth

(1770–1850)

When 'Kubla Khan' was first published, Coleridge attached a note explaining that the poem was the result of a dream he had experienced after an 'anodyne' he had taken had caused him to fall asleep in his chair. On awaking, he had 'a distinct recollection' of having composed 'from two to three hundred lines', of which he wrote down the fifty-four lines of the published poem before a 'person on business from Porlock' came to his door and called him away. When he returned he found that 'all the rest had passed away like the images on the surface of a stream into which a stone has been cast'. A century and a half later, the English poet Stevie Smith was sceptical about his claim. In her poem 'Thoughts about the Person from Porlock' she concluded, 'the truth is I think he was already stuck / With Kubla Khan'.

Five miles meandering with a mazy motion

Through wood and dale the sacred river ran,

Then reached the caverns measureless to man,

And sank in tumult to a lifeless ocean:

And 'mid this tumult Kubla heard from far

Ancestral voices prophesying war!

FROM 'KUBLA KHAN', BY

Samuel Taylor Coleridge

(1772–1834)

George Byron was three years old when his father died, leaving nothing but debts, and he was ten when his great-uncle 'The Wicked Lord' also died so that he inherited the barony that gave him his title. After an unhappy childhood spent in poverty and marred by a deformity of the foot, Byron arrived at Cambridge University, where he began to reinvent himself as the figure we now think of as a 'Byronic hero'. He met Lady Caroline Lamb, the wife of the future Lord Melbourne, who described him as 'mad, bad and dangerous to know'; he gave a much-admired speech in the House of Lords; and the publication of his epic poem 'Childe Harold's Pilgrimage' allowed him to write, 'I awoke ... and found myself famous.' At nearly the same time he began a love affair with his half-sister Augusta (the offspring of his late father's first marriage), and agreed to marry a cousin of Lady Melbourne, Annabella Milbanke, even though 'never had lover been less in haste to greet his bride'. The marriage soon ended, amid rumours and scandal, and Byron left for the continent, never to return; he died in Greece eight years later as a hero of the Greek resistance to Turkish rule. His daughter, Ada, grew up to be a mathematician and a pioneer of computer science.

I would to Heaven that I were so much clay,
　　As I am blood, bone, marrow, passion, feeling –
Because at least the past were passed away,
　　And for the future – (but I write this reeling,
Having got drunk exceedingly to-day,
　　So that I seem to stand upon the ceiling)
I say – the future is a serious matter –
　　And so – for God's sake – hock and soda-water!

FROM 'DON JUAN', BY

Lord Byron

(1788–1824)

After being expelled from University College, Oxford, in his first year, Shelley moved to London and became involved in social and political causes. He met the radical social philosopher William Godwin, and soon eloped to Europe with Godwin's daughter Mary Wollstonecraft Godwin and her stepsister Claire Clairmont, who was obsessed with Lord Byron. In Geneva Mary wrote a novel called *Frankenstein, or The Modern Prometheus*, while Claire was pregnant with Byron's daughter Allegra. Shelley's radical political views are apparent in the lines quoted, which express his contempt for the British royal family; in his essay 'A Defence of Poetry', he declared that 'Poets are the unacknowledged legislators of the world'. To Byron, Shelley seemed a 'crank and enthusiast', 'shrill-voiced, untidy, with glittering eyes', and he gave him the nickname of 'The Snake', but though they had their disagreements, they remained friends. They had spent a Sunday in one another's company with Leigh Hunt at Pisa when Shelley and two others set out in a small boat bound for Lerici, where the Shelleys were living, only to be swallowed up and drowned in a violent storm. Byron watched as Shelley's body was cremated in a funeral pyre on the beach at La Spezia, and saw the brains boiling in the broken skull, then stripped and swam out to his anchored yacht.

An old, mad, blind, despised, and dying king –

Princes, the dregs of their dull race, who flow

Through public scorn – mud from a muddy spring;

Rulers who neither see, nor feel, nor know,

FROM 'ENGLAND IN 1819', BY

Percy Bysshe Shelley

(1792–1822)

When Keats was dying of consumption in a room beside the Spanish Steps in Rome, he asked that his gravestone be inscribed with the words 'Here lies one whose name was writ in water'. His early death inspired a major poem by Shelley, 'Adonais' ('Forget the Past, his fate and fame shall be / An echo and a light unto eternity!'), while Byron added, in a letter to his publisher, 'Who killed John Keats? / "I," says the Quarterly, / So savage and Tartarly; / ""Twas one of my feats"'. An unfavourable review in a literary journal has not been shown by medical science to have a link with tuberculosis, and Byron wrote to Shelley, 'I am very sorry to hear what you say of Keats — is it actually true? I did not think criticism had been so killing.' At least Shelley was right about his fame; though Keats only had time to write fifty-four poems before he died, his belief, expressed in a letter to his brother, that 'I think I shall be among the English Poets after my death' proved correct.

Season of mists and mellow fruitfulness,

Close bosom-friend of the maturing sun;

Conspiring with him how to load and bless

With fruit the vines that round the thatch-eaves run;

FROM 'TO AUTUMN', BY

John Keats

(1795–1821)

The shot referred to was the first in the American Revolution, which led to a group of British colonies gaining their independence as the United States of America. Emerson's phrase has since been applied by other writers to many opening moments, and used to describe both cannon fire and golf shots. Emerson was born in Boston, the son of a minister, and became a pastor in the Unitarian Church before his opinions led to his resignation. He is best known as a prose writer and philosopher, but his interest in poetry was such that in 1833 he travelled to England and met William Wordsworth and Samuel Taylor Coleridge.

By the rude bridge that arched the flood,

Their flag to April's breeze unfurled,

Here once the embattled farmers stood

And fired the shot heard round the world.

FROM 'CONCORD HYMN', BY

Ralph Waldo Emerson

(1803–1882)

When Elizabeth Barrett was a teenager, she damaged her spine in an accident, and for many years she lived as an invalid under the eyes of her over-protective father. She was a prolific and successful writer nonetheless, and at the age of forty she met the poet Robert Browning, six years her junior, and eloped with him to Italy, where her strength revived to the extent that she was able to give birth to a son and to write her best-known books, *Sonnets From the Portuguese* and *Aurora Leigh*. Her work was more highly regarded, by the time she died in Florence in her fifties, than that of her husband.

How do I love thee? Let me count the ways.

I love thee to the depth and breadth and height

My soul can reach, when feeling out of sight

For the ends of Being and ideal Grace.

FROM 'SONNETS FROM THE PORTUGUESE', BY

Elizabeth Barrett Browning

(1806–1861)

Though Longfellow's reputation has declined since the days of his fame, when the international success of 'The Song of Hiawatha' helped to begin the process by which American popular culture has come to dominate the world, he can still be admired for his technical facility, and for the way in which his poetry's rhythms have insinuated themselves into the ear of many a reader. Philip Larkin noticed that his well-known poem 'The Explosion' was written in the metre of 'Hiawatha', though he had not intended it. Longfellow was a professor of languages and literature at Harvard, but the success of his writing was such that he was able to retire in his forties. In 1861 his second wife was burned to death when her dress caught fire.

Ye who love a nation's legends,

Love the ballads of a people,

That like voices from afar off

Call to us to pause and listen,

Speak in tones so plain and childlike

Scarcely can the ear distinguish

Whether they are sung or spoken; –

Listen to this Indian legend,

To this song of Hiawatha!

FROM 'THE SONG OF HIAWATHA', BY

Henry Wadsworth Longfellow

(1807–1882)

Though it purports to be a translation from the Arabic, FitzGerald's version of *The Rubaiyat* takes so many liberties that it is generally regarded as an original poem in its own right. The poem itself is a mix of memorable, much-quoted phrases, genuine insights and utter banalities. FitzGerald was educated at Trinity College, Cambridge, where he knew Tennyson and Thackeray, and then pursued a quiet life devoted to study and translation from many languages.

The Moving Finger writes; and, having writ,

Moves on: nor all your Piety nor Wit

   Shall lure it back to cancel half a Line,

Nor all your Tears wash out a Word of it.

FROM *THE RUBAIYAT OF OMAR KHAYYAM OF NAISHAPUR*, BY

Edward FitzGerald

(1809–1883)

Alfred Tennyson was educated at Trinity College, Cambridge, where he knew Thackeray, Edward FitzGerald, and AH Hallam, the subject of his *In Memoriam AHH*, the poetic sequence that brought Tennyson fame. That fame only arrived after his first two published books – which contain some of the finest poems in the English language, including 'The Lady of Shalott' and 'The Lotos-eaters' – were dismissed by critics. His third book established his reputation in 1842, and when the Poet Laureate, William Wordsworth, died in 1850, the year *In Memoriam* was published, Tennyson was appointed in his place and became such a favourite of Queen Victoria that he was elevated to the barony. Long after his death his grandson the Honourable Lionel Tennyson became captain of the English cricket team, and faced up as heroically as the members of the Light Brigade to the bombardment of the Australian fast bowlers Jack Gregory and Ted MacDonald.

The woods decay, the woods decay and fall,

The vapours weep their burthen to the ground,

Man comes and tills the field and lies beneath,

And after many a summer dies the swan.

FROM 'TITHONUS', BY

Alfred, Lord Tennyson

(1809–1892)

Browning's poem quoted here is, like much of his work, full of exclamations ('G-r-r-r', 'Whew', 'he-he'), expletives and colloquialisms, and yet all of this is contained in perfectly regular rhyming verse. As a young writer, Browning produced several dramas, though these are not performed anymore, and the experience gave him the idea of writing poems that are dramatic monologues, uttered by characters or personae who are not the author himself. The idea was an influential one, and was taken up by twentieth-century writers such as Ezra Pound and TS Eliot, who also adopted Browning's incorporation of everyday speech into serious poetry. After his elopement with Elizabeth Barrett, Browning lived in Italy until her death fifteen years later; he then returned to England with their son, who grew up to become a sculptor.

G-r-r-r – there go, my heart's abhorrence!

Water your damned flower-pots, do!

If hate killed men, Brother Lawrence,

God's blood, would not mine kill you!

FROM 'SOLILOQUY OF THE SPANISH CLOISTER', BY

Robert Browning

(1812–1889)

Free verse, or poetry without metre, rhyme or regular line-length, was not unknown in English literature by the beginning of the nineteenth century, as such writing existed as far back as the Psalms and the Song of Solomon in the Bible, while more recent versions of it could be seen in the works of Christopher Smart and William Blake. But it took the example of Walt Whitman to liberate poets, not only in America but all over the world, from the constraining rules of traditional prosody. Thus, Whitman was even more influential than Browning on the poets who followed him, even though a critic remarked of his work that he was 'as unacquainted with art as a hog is with mathematics'. Whitman left school at the age of eleven, and was largely self-educated; he worked at many occupations, including printer, teacher, journalist and civil servant, and during the Civil War he acted for a time as a nurse. The war inspired one of his most famous poems, 'O Captain! My Captain!', about the death of Abraham Lincoln, which he wrote in regular rhyming verse.

I celebrate myself, and sing myself,

And what I assume you shall assume,

For every atom belonging to me as good belongs to you.

FROM 'SONG OF MYSELF', BY

Walt Whitman

(1819–1892)

Matthew Arnold was the son of Dr Thomas Arnold, headmaster of Rugby, the famous school where the game of rugby football was first played, and he grew up in a large family where writing was a natural amusement and Wordsworth was a family friend. Arnold was educated at Balliol College, Oxford, and worked for many years as an inspector of schools; he was elected Professor of Poetry at Oxford University at the age of thirty-five. The memorable image at the end of 'Dover Beach' has a sense of universality about it, and could perhaps refer to any conflict, but in fact Arnold, who was a classicist, was referring to a specific battle described by Thucydides, which was fought at night so that 'the two sides could not distinguish friend from foe' – hence the ignorance.

And we are here as on a darkling plain

Swept with confused alarms of struggle and flight,

Where ignorant armies clash by night.

FROM 'DOVER BEACH', BY

Matthew Arnold

(1822–1888)

Emily Dickinson was born in Amherst, Massachusetts, and, except for one year at a seminary, did not leave her family's home. She lived as a hermit in her room, writing letters and poems and seldom venturing outside; it was a life so uneventful that one would scarcely expect it to become the subject of a movie, as it did in 2016. Though Dickinson wrote nearly two thousand poems, hardly any of them were published in her lifetime; her sister released a selection of them after her death, and ever since then more editions, and versions, of her work have been discovered by scholars and literary detectives. Her deceptively simple style derives from the rhythms of the hymn-book, though her method of punctuation was all her own (her earliest editors tried to eliminate her idiosyncrasies). The content of her poems is profound, and at times terrifying. Her most productive years of writing coincided with the American Civil War, yet the poems written at this time make no allusion to those dramatic events.

Because I could not stop for Death –

He kindly stopped for me –

The Carriage held but just Ourselves –

And Immortality.

FROM *POEM 712*, BY

Emily Dickinson

(1830–1886)

Hardy was one of the great novelists of the nineteenth century, and one of the great poets of the twentieth century. Yet he did not set out with high ambitions; he only hoped to prove himself 'a good hand at a serial', and most of his fourteen novels were first published in serial form in magazines such as the *Cornhill*, edited by Virginia Woolf's father, Leslie Stephen. The success of those novels was such that Hardy was able to retire and devote the rest of his life to poetry, producing an extraordinary body of work, technically skilful and varied, full of memorable images and phrases, and, despite some occasionally archaic language, very up to date – some of his more than 900 poems touch on contemporary matters such as the sinking of the *Titanic*, the First World War and the theories of Einstein. The lines quoted here appear to have been the inspiration for the Australian poet David Campbell's poem 'Mothers and Daughters': 'The cruel girls we loved / Are over forty, / Their subtle daughters / Have stolen their beauty; / And with a blue stare/ Of cool surprise, / They mock their anxious mothers / With their mothers' eyes'.

These market-dames, mid-aged, with lips thin-drawn,

　And tissues sere,

Are they the ones we loved in years agone,

　And courted here?

FROM 'FORMER BEAUTIES', BY

Thomas Hardy

(1840–1928)

Hopkins was educated at Highgate School in London, where he knew Marcus Clarke, who was to become a celebrated novelist in Australia; he then studied classics at Balliol College, Oxford, where he met the future British Poet Laureate Robert Bridges, as well as EH Coleridge, grandson of the poet, and JH Newman, who assisted his conversion to Catholicism. Hopkins became a Jesuit priest, and at first abandoned his plan to become a poet or a painter; but the church hierarchy encouraged him to return to writing, and he proceeded to develop radical theories about techniques of versification, including his notion of 'sprung rhythm', while producing a body of work that had a profound influence on many of the poets of the twentieth century. He did not publish his poetry in his lifetime, but sent copies of everything he wrote to Bridges, who released a selection of Hopkins' poems nearly thirty years after his death.

Cloud-puffball, torn tufts, tossed pillows
　　flaunt forth, then chevy on an air-
built thoroughfare: heaven-roysterers, in gay-gangs
　　they throng; they glitter in marches.
Down roughcast, down dazzling whitewash,
　　wherever an elm arches,
Shivelights and shadowtackle in long
　　lashes lace, lance, and pair.

FROM 'THAT NATURE IS A HERACLITEAN FIRE AND
OF THE COMFORT OF THE RESURRECTION', BY

Gerard Manley Hopkins

(1844–1889)

The fourth line of this short poem became a catchphrase for anti-war movements everywhere, especially after the Second World War. It derives from a classical inscription at Thermopylae in Greece, and can be seen in another version in a poem by AD Hope ('We took their orders and are dead.') After failing his degree at St John's College, Oxford, Housman worked for ten years in the Patent Office in London while continuing to write and publish papers about the classics as an unattached scholar. At the age of thirty-three he was appointed Professor of Classics at University College, London, and later he became a professor at Trinity College, Cambridge. His exquisite and economical poems only appeared at long intervals. His first collection, *A Shropshire Lad*, was first published in 1896 at the author's expense, but it became immensely popular among British soldiers of the First World War.

These, in the day when heaven was falling,

The hour when earth's foundations fled,

Followed their mercenary calling

And took their wages and are dead.

FROM 'EPITAPH ON AN ARMY OF MERCENARIES', BY

AE Housman

(1859–1936)

I n these few short lines, excerpted from a short poem, there are no fewer than seven phrases that have become a familiar part of our vocabulary, whether being used as book titles or newspaper headings. Perhaps more significantly, these lines read today as if they referred to the current state of the world, even though they were written in 1921. Yeats was the son of an artist, and studied art, as did his brother, the painter Jack B Yeats, before he turned to poetry; he may be the greatest of all the many fine poets who have emerged from Ireland. For much of his life he benefited from the patronage of Lady Augusta Gregory, with whom he founded the Irish National Theatre, and whose great-grandson, William De Winton, subsequently moved to Australia to start a bookshop. In later life Yeats became a senator in the Irish Free State, and described himself as 'a sixty-year-old smiling public man'.

Things fall apart, the centre cannot hold;

Mere anarchy is loosed upon the world,

The blood-dimmed tide is loosed, and everywhere

The ceremony of innocence is drowned;

The best lack all conviction, while the worst

Are full of passionate intensity.

FROM 'THE SECOND COMING', BY

William Butler Yeats

(1865–1939)

Brennan was the first Australian-born poet to see himself as part of the international poetry-writing community. He had lived in Berlin as a graduate student, and married the daughter of his German landlady, before becoming Professor of German and Comparative Literature at Sydney University. He corresponded with the French poet Stéphane Mallarmé, and some of his poems show the influence of the French Symbolists, who would also influence TS Eliot. Unfortunately, Brennan's most ambitious works are his weakest. A fatal weakness for alcohol led to his dismissal from his academic position and his early death. In his poverty-stricken last years he encountered the young AD Hope in front of a hotel urinal, and completed a Latin tag that Hope had inscribed on the wall before him.

If questioning could make us wise
no eyes would ever gaze in eyes;
if all our tale were told in speech
no mouths would wander each to each.

FROM 'BECAUSE SHE WOULD ASK ME
WHY I LOVED HER', BY

Christopher Brennan

(1870–1932)

Frost had known little but failure when he moved to England, from New England, in his late thirties. He had been a teacher, a mill hand and a journalist, and his attempts to become a farmer had been unsuccessful, while his poetry remained unpublished. In England he made the acquaintance of Edward Thomas, Rupert Brooke and Ezra Pound, among others, and with their encouragement and promotion published his first two books in London. The second of these, North of Boston (1914), made him the most celebrated American poet of his generation, and he remained a revered figure for the rest of his life. Frost had first written poems in the nineteenth century, yet he lived long enough to be invited to recite his work at the inauguration of President John F Kennedy in 1961, where he became, like many poets of an earlier age from Marvell to Tennyson, a courtier of his nation's ruler.

Two roads diverged in a wood, and I –

I took the one less traveled by,

And that has made all the difference.

FROM 'THE ROAD NOT TAKEN', BY

Robert Frost

(1874–1963)

Thomas was a hard-working journeyman writer, biographer and book reviewer, with a growing family to support, when, at the age of thirty-six, he met an American visitor to England, Robert Frost, who encouraged him to start writing poetry, just as Thomas had encouraged Frost's poetry. Soon afterwards Thomas enlisted in the Artists Rifles, and he wrote most of his poetry while he was a serviceman. Before he had a chance to see it published in book form, however, he was killed at the Battle of Arras. In his three short years as a practising poet, Thomas produced a highly original body of work, using everyday language and conventional forms to explore the depths behind the commonplace and in nature, just as Frost was to do.

Yes, I remember Adlestrop –

The name, because one afternoon

Of heat the express-train drew up there

Unwontedly. It was late June.

FROM 'ADLESTROP', BY

Edward Thomas

(1878–1917)

Stevens' elaborate, foreign-sounding language, cryptic images and tone of emotional detachment inspired a generation of imitators (the best known being the New York poet John Ashbery) to write poems with attention-grabbing yet opaque surfaces over a seeming absence of subject or content. Yet the poems Stevens himself wrote are never devoid of meaning, even if readers at times must work hard to discern it. Those poems might convey the impression that their author was a flamboyant, bohemian figure, but in fact he was the opposite: he trained as a lawyer, then worked all his life for an insurance company, rising to become its vice-president. He wrote, in another poem, 'The only emperor is the emperor of ice-cream.'

Complacencies of the peignoir, and late

Coffee and oranges in a sunny chair,

And the green freedom of a cockatoo

FROM 'SUNDAY MORNING', BY

Wallace Stevens

(1879–1955)

'No ideas but in things' was among the various and sometimes contradictory statements Williams made to justify his poetic practice, and it does summarise the effect some of his best-known poems have, presenting everyday objects without comment or elaboration. The simplicity and directness of his diction, and the unregulated freedom of his verse forms, have made him one of the most influential writers of the past century, imitated by generations. Williams graduated in medicine from the University of Pennsylvania, and worked all his life as a pediatrician, writing poems in his surgery between appointments and after work. He also made the acquaintance of most of the major writers of his time, from Pound, Eliot and James Joyce to Robert Lowell and Allen Ginsberg. WH Auden's 'Musee des Beaux Arts' is a version of the poem quoted here, in regular rhymes rather than Williams' stepped-down free-verse line.

unsignificantly

off the coast

there was

a splash quite unnoticed

this was

Icarus drowning

FROM 'LANDSCAPE WITH THE FALL OF ICARUS', BY

William Carlos Williams

(1883–1963)

Like Thomas Hardy, Lawrence achieved greatness both as poet and novelist, and like his near-contemporaries Ezra Pound and TS Eliot he spent most of his life abroad. His early writing was encouraged by Ford Madox Ford, but after the success of his first novel he encountered Frieda von Richthofen, the wife of a German professor and cousin of the future war pilot Manfred von Richthofen (the 'Red Baron'), and sent her a note saying 'You are the most wonderful woman in England'. She replied, 'How do you know?' They eloped to Europe, only returning to England, where several of his books were prosecuted for obscenity, for the duration of the First World War. They then went to Italy, to New Mexico in the USA, and to Australia, where they lived for three months and Lawrence wrote the novel *Kangaroo* as well a poem called 'Kangaroo', before returning to Italy. Their last move was to Vence, close to Nice in France, where Lawrence died of consumption.

The Italians vulgarly say, it stands for the female part;

   the fig-fruit:

The fissure, the yoni,

The wonderful moist conductivity towards the centre.

FROM 'FIGS', BY

DH Lawrence

(1885–1930)

'I make a pact with you, Walt Whitman', the brash young Pound wrote, 'Let there be commerce between us'. No-one did more than Pound to learn from, and to extend, the example of literary innovation set by Whitman, not only in his own work but in that of many others. Pound was raised in Philadelphia, and studied languages at the University of Pennsylvania, but it was not enough for him to become a successful American poet like his life-long friend William Carlos Williams. In 1908 he moved to London and became secretary to WB Yeats, and, while encouraging and promoting such writers as Robert Frost, Edward Thomas, TS Eliot, HD, James Joyce, Ernest Hemingway and Ford Madox Ford, made himself into a major international figure. In 1924 he moved to Italy, where he met a bemused Benito Mussolini and became a supporter of fascism. For many years Pound worked on his 'Cantos', which are full of beautiful passages but are yet so incoherent as to suggest the work of a madman. That suggestion saved Pound's life when he was captured by American forces at the end of the Second World War and charged with treason: instead of being given a death sentence, he was committed to St Elizabeth's Hospital for the Criminally Insane for thirteen years.

The ant's a centaur in his dragon world.

Pull down thy vanity, it is not man

Made courage, or made order, or made grace,

Pull down thy vanity, I say pull down.

FROM 'CANTO LXXXI', BY

Ezra Pound

(1885–1972)

Before the First World War, Sassoon already had somewhat of a reputation as a poet and man of letters in the fashionable 'Georgian' style of the time, but his first-hand experience of war after he enlisted in the Royal Welsh Fusiliers changed both his writing and his character. He began to write directly, and in plain, conversational language, about the horrors he had witnessed, and he became publicly opposed to the war, which had in the meantime led to him being hospitalised with 'shell shock'. In hospital he met Wilfred Owen, whose work followed a similar trajectory, though Owen's writing has greater literary power. The poem quoted from here refers to the battle at which Edward Thomas (see page 88) was killed.

'He's a cheery old card,' grunted Harry to Jack

As they slogged up to Arras with rifle and pack.

But he did for them both by his plan of attack.

FROM 'THE GENERAL', BY

Siegfried Sassoon

(1886–1967)

In old age, Moore was such a celebrated figure in American culture that she was asked to give a name to a new model Ford; she was invited to throw the first pitch in baseball's World Series and attended Dodgers games with George Plimpton and Robert Lowell; and she even collaborated on a poem with Muhammad Ali (she suggested the title 'A Poem on the Annihilation of Ernie Terrell'). It would seem improbable for such a character, a tiny woman often dressed in a bushy fur coat and a tricorne hat who lived for much of her life with her mother, to attain such renown, as the poetry she wrote was challenging and original, if highly disciplined – William Carlos Williams compared her poems to Picasso's Cubist portraits. Using the rhythms of everyday speech rather than any conventional poetic metre, Moore constructed intricate stanza forms, sometimes rhymed and sometimes not, whose length was determined by counting syllables, and with the fastidious attention to detail of a zoologist (she had studied biology at Bryn Mawr) she described animals and the natural world in a way that would later be recalled in the work of her protégée and friend Elizabeth Bishop.

I, too, dislike it: there are things that are

important beyond all this fiddle.

Reading it, however, with a perfect contempt for it,

one discovers in it after all, a place for the genuine.

FROM 'POETRY', BY

Marianne Moore

(1887–1972)

Pound and Eliot, both of them Americans, were the two most influential presences in English poetry in the first half of the twentieth century. Both were distinguished scholars and exceptionally well read in several languages. It was Eliot who first displayed what was to become one of the most characteristic strategies of modernist poetry, the extensive use of quotations from, and references to, other poets in his own poems, so that 'The Waste Land' amounts almost to a verbal collage of classical and Shakespearean phrases. The poem's opening lines, quoted here, refer to the opening of Chaucer's *Canterbury Tales* (see page 6). Pound, whose editing skills had much to do with the success of 'The Waste Land', was to use the same method throughout his 'Cantos', but while Pound retained his American accent and character, Eliot did not, coming to resemble the archetypal English gentleman with his elaborate courtesy (in evidence in his letters) and an exaggerated English accent (which can be heard in recordings of his voice).

April is the cruellest month, breeding

Lilacs out of the dead land, mixing

Memory and desire, stirring

Dull roots with spring rain.

FROM 'THE WASTE LAND', BY

TS Eliot

(1888–1965)

I n the First World War, Matthews fought for the Australian army at Gallipoli and in France, and the best of his poems about the first-hand experience of war are as powerful and technically innovative as the works of Owen, Graves and Sassoon. Unlike Wilfred Owen and Edward Thomas, Matthews survived the war, and returned to Australia to establish a vineyard at Moorebank, just outside Sydney. Kenneth Slessor's famous poem 'Five Bells' refers to a visit to the vineyard, which became a meeting place for writers and artists. In the Second World War Matthews was falsely accused of disloyalty and imprisoned for six months, during which time his vineyard was ruined by neglect. He was later awarded compensation by a Royal Commission and cleared of any wrongdoing.

They said there was a woman in the hills

Behind us. All day long she watched for when

A man's head showed.

       Some knew that she was young

And beautiful. And some that she was old,

Mad with a hate of men.

'Each shot she fires kills,'

They said.

FROM 'WOMEN ARE NOT GENTLEMEN', BY

Harley Matthews

(1889–1968)

O f all the poets whose work emerged from the First World War, Owen was the most gifted, so that his death in the trenches a week before the end of the war was bitterly ironic. He was only twenty-two when he enlisted in the Artists' Rifles, and he fought heroically, eventually winning the Military Cross, even as he was becoming disillusioned with the whole process of war. Temporarily invalided out of the front lines, he was sent to the same hospital as Siegfried Sassoon and Robert Graves, and was encouraged by them to write more directly about his experience of the war. At the same time he was a considerable literary innovator, using half rhymes in his poems in a way that had not been seen before, and inspiring many imitators. In a preface to the collection of his poems that was published after his death he remarked, 'Above all I am not concerned with Poetry. My subject is War, and the pity of War. The Poetry is in the pity'.

What passing-bells for these who die as cattle?

– Only the monstrous anger of the guns.

FROM 'ANTHEM FOR DOOMED YOUTH', BY

Wilfred Owen

(1893–1918)

Graves had barely left school when he joined the British Expeditionary Force and went to France to fight in the First World War; he was not yet twenty-one when he was reported dead and was able to read his own obituary in the London *Times*. Wounded and suffering from shell shock, he was sent to the same hospital as Siegfried Sassoon and Wilfred Owen. He published a prose memoir, *Goodbye to All That*, about his wartime experiences, but suppressed his poems on the subject because he regarded them as inferior to Sassoon's and Owen's war poetry. In fact, they were not. Later, he had a long association with the American poet Laura Riding, which led to his unusual theories about the feminine muse and his book on the subject, *The White Goddess*. He also wrote the classically inspired novel *I, Claudius*, living long enough to see his fiction adapted as a popular television series.

Why have such scores of lovely, gifted girls

Married impossible men?

FROM 'A SLICE OF WEDDING CAKE', BY

Robert Graves

(1895–1985)

At the outset of the First World War, Kenneth Adolph Schloesser's father changed his Germanic family name to the Anglicised 'Slessor'. Between the two wars, Slessor worked as a journalist while writing all of the poems on which his reputation as Australia's finest poet rests. With the publication of 'Five Bells' in 1939, he felt he had nothing more to say as a poet, though his life as writer and editor continued. In the Second World War he became an Official War Correspondent with the Australian army, and the lines quoted come from a poem that emerged from that experience. It was the only poem written in his later years that he considered complete: it shows the feeling for rhythm and assonance typical of his strongest earlier work. After he ceased writing serious poetry, Slessor often produced witty occasional verse in letters, newspaper columns, and even in the actor Chips Rafferty's visitors' book.

Softly and humbly to the Gulf of Arabs

The convoys of dead sailors come;

At night they sway and wander in the waters far under,

But morning rolls them in the foam.

FROM 'BEACH BURIAL', BY

Kenneth Slessor

(1901–1971)

Born in New York State, Nash attended Harvard University for just one year then worked as a teacher, a bond salesman, an advertising writer and a book publisher before joining the staff of the recently founded *New Yorker* magazine. His immensely popular humorous verse contributed to the early success of that now venerable journal; his style was described as 'talking uncommon good sense while apparently playing the fool'. The technique he relied on involved attaching comically surprising rhymes to the end of long prosaic lines, while his content comprised both a clear-eyed vision of the mundane details of contemporary life and an incongruous interest in literature and the classics, so that many of Nash's poems include insightful comments on writers from Shakespeare to his contemporaries.

To be grateful for small favours I am nothing loath,

Wherefore I have been recently counting my blessings,

employing for the

purpose the fingers of a three-toed sloth.

FROM 'WE PAUSE NOW BRIEFLY FOR AN
IMPORTANT MESSAGE', BY

Ogden Nash

(1902–1971)

Betjeman was considered unfit for service in the armed forces during the Second World War, but many of his poems have a military presence, whether of a subaltern, a captain, Major Maxton-Weir of this poem, some 'beefy ATS' or 'Clemency the General's daughter'. Betjeman also wrote the heartfelt plea 'Come, friendly bombs, and fall on Slough / It isn't fit for humans now'. Few English poets have been less influential than him, because his style is inimitable, and nobody has been more popular with readers – his book sales outstripped those of Byron, who was distributed by the same publishing firm as Betjeman more than a century earlier. Like Tennyson, Betjeman became the Poet Laureate, as well as being a television personality and a public figure so loved that he caused the nation to hold its breath when he was taken to hospital; he revived when his childhood teddy bear, Archibald, was brought to his bedside. Gavin Ewart, one of his greatest admirers, wrote a poem called 'Rush that Bear' about this incident.

Ting-a-ling the telephone, to-whit to-whoo the owls,

Judy, Judy, Judy girl, and have you fed the fowls?

No answer as the poultry gate is swinging there ajar.

Boom the bombers overhead, between the clouds a star,

And just outside, among the arks,

in a shadowy sheltered place

Lie Judy and a paratroop in horrible embrace.

FROM 'INVASION EXERCISE ON THE
POULTRY FARM', BY

John Betjeman

(1906–1984)

These lines were removed from later reprints of this poem, as Auden in his maturity came to feel that many of the memorable rhetorical phrases in his youthful work (such as 'The conscious acceptance of guilt in the necessary murder' in his poem 'Spain 1937') were essentially dishonest. Yet the point he makes, here, about the lasting effect of writing well, is still valid, and has not been expressed better. He also cut from this poem the lines that claim that time 'Worships language and forgives / Everyone by whom it lives'. As a precocious young man, Auden became the foremost representative of a group of English poets of the 1930s that also included Louis MacNeice, Stephen Spender and Cecil Day-Lewis. They wrote politically engaged verse that leaned to the left in the days when the nature of communism in Russia was not fully known. The Second World War changed their views, and Auden in particular turned from politics to religion. Though the poems of his later years are as skilful and witty as any of his earlier works, many readers still prefer his memorable early poems for all their 'dishonest' rhetoric – for time has pardoned not only Yeats, Kipling and Claudel, but also Auden himself.

Time that with this strange excuse

Pardoned Kipling and his views,

And will pardon Paul Claudel,

Pardons him for writing well

FROM 'IN MEMORY OF WB YEATS', BY

WH Auden

(1907–1973)

There was a time when every Australian poet attempted a definitive summary of the country they had been born in; Hope's version of this exercise is the most successful, and the most quoted. Phrases from this poem, such as 'From deserts the prophets come', have been used as book titles and have entered our language. Hope lived an uneventful life as an academic, becoming Professor of English at the Australian National University, where a building was named in his honour while he was still working in it; at one stage subversive students used spray paint to rename it the 'AD Dope Building'.

They call her a young country, but they lie:
She is the last of lands, the emptiest,
A woman beyond her change of life, a breast
Still tender but within the womb is dry.

FROM 'AUSTRALIA', BY

AD Hope

(1907-2000)

Early in his career the Irishman MacNeice was closely associated with WH Auden, Stephen Spender and Cecil Day-Lewis, prompting the South African poet Roy Campbell to invent a composite poet called 'MacSpaunday'. MacNeice travelled to Iceland with Auden, and both produced some memorable work about the experience, incompatible with one another though they were. MacNeice had met Auden at Merton College, Oxford, where he also knew Betjeman; he subsequently became a radio producer at the BBC. He was a prolific poet who has been underrated in comparison with his celebrated contemporaries; his poems are remarkable for their clarity and technical skill. A liking for alcohol contributed to his early demise.

And when the night came down upon the bogland

   With all-enveloping wings

The coal-black turfstacks rose against the darkness

   Like the tombs of nameless kings.

FROM 'SLIGO AND MAYO', BY

Louis MacNeice

(1907–1963)

Spender's most famous single line seems to sum up the career of a man whose life was dedicated to name-dropping, though this is not entirely fair to him. If he was the least gifted of the 'MacSpaunday' group of poets, he worked hard all his life on behalf of other writers, as an editor and promoter and as a member of associations such as PEN. In the 1930s he was a dedicated and earnest communist; by the 1950s he was editor of *Encounter*, the anti-communist magazine supported by the Congress for Cultural Freedom, an organisation set up and funded by the CIA. Spender lived long enough to see his daughter Lizzie marry one who is 'truly great', the Australian writer and performer Barry Humphries.

I think continually of those who were truly great

FROM 'I THINK CONTINUALLY ...', BY

Stephen Spender

(1909–1995)

Effectively orphaned by the age of five, when her widowed mother was removed to a mental hospital, Bishop was raised by grandparents and aunts before, as a student at Vassar, she met Marianne Moore, who became an unlikely maternal figure and lifelong mentor. When Bishop's first book, *North and South*, was published in 1946, Moore, in a review, praised it for 'the flicker of impudence'. Bishop was said to be highly attractive to both men and women, but she preferred women; despite this fact, Robert Lowell proposed marriage to her during one of his manic phases. For many years she lived in Brazil, and she travelled widely before spending her final years teaching at Harvard University. Though she benefited from Moore's mentorship, she was a very different poet, even when dealing with similar subjects.

– Even losing you (the joking voice, a gesture

I love) I shan't have lied. It's evident

the art of losing's not too hard to master

though it may look like (Write it!) like disaster.

FROM 'ONE ART', BY

Elizabeth Bishop

(1911–1979)

The experiences that Jarrell had after he enlisted in the US army in the Second World War affected him so much that his death – it seems he walked into speeding traffic at night – was almost certainly a suicide. Yet some of his most impressive poetry emerged from those same experiences. He taught at several universities and colleges, including Kenyon College, where he shared a room with Robert Lowell, and he came to be more highly regarded as a critic than as a poet, notorious for his witty dismissals of writers he did not admire, though his positive assessments of rising figures such as William Carlos Williams, Elizabeth Bishop and Lowell helped to create their reputations. His prose collection *Poetry and the Age* justifies Lowell's description of him as 'the best critic of my generation'.

Six miles from earth, loosed from its dream of life,

I woke to black flak and the nightmare fighters.

When I died they washed me out of the turret with a hose.

FROM 'THE DEATH OF THE BALL TURRET
GUNNER', BY

Randall Jarrell

(1914–1965)

More than half of the poems that would make Thomas famous were composed between the ages of eighteen and twenty; in the second half of his abbreviated life he devoted much of his literary talent to writing begging letters to friends and wealthy patrons alike. From an early age, Thomas sought to live a poet's life on the Byronic model of dissolution, even though his somewhat delicate physique was unsuited to dissipation. His early poems have a powerful rhythmic effect, but defy understanding; his later ones, crafted at a slow and painstaking rate, are less obscure but excessively wordy. During the Second World War he wrote radio scripts for the BBC, and recordings of his voice show that he was a gifted actor; after the war, he toured America repeatedly, playing the part of the dissolute poet and giving well-attended poetry readings. His fame was such, especially after his death, that a young American musician with literary pretensions called Robert Zimmerman changed his surname to 'Dylan'. Thomas's then uncommon Welsh Christian name is now one of the most popular of baby names. Thomas and his wife Caitlin (another popular name now) had three children; their son Llewelyn later migrated to Australia.

Oh as I was young and easy in the mercy of his means,
Time held me green and dying
Though I sang in my chains like the sea.

FROM 'FERN HILL', BY

Dylan Thomas

(1914–1953)

Wright was born into a wealthy farming family and grew up near Armidale in New South Wales; she attended Sydney University without graduating before she travelled in England and Europe in the late 1930s. She returned to work on the family property when the Second World War caused a labour shortage. Her first published book, *The Moving Image* (1946), established her reputation as one of Australia's most accomplished poets. She married JP McKinney, a philosopher and writer more than two decades her senior, and came to be influenced by his ideas, to the detriment of her poetry. As she grew older she became increasingly deaf, which may have affected her poetic ear. In later years she took up political causes, in particular Aboriginal Land Rights, as a result of her friendship with the senior civil servant HC Coombs, who also encouraged her to move from Armidale to Braidwood near Canberra.

South of my days' circle, part of my blood's country,

rises that tableland, high delicate outline

of bony slopes wincing under the winter,

low trees blue-leaved and olive, outcropping granite –

FROM 'SOUTH OF MY DAYS', BY

Judith Wright

(1915–2000)

This short poem concludes 'But what made him do it? That is very far from a laughing matter'. Ewart's poems are full of laughter otherwise. He first emerged as a published poet as a seventeen-year-old schoolboy, and was in his early twenties when his first book, *Poems and Songs*, was published in 1939. He served in the British army in the Second World War and wrote very little for the next twenty-five years, during which time he was known mainly for a little poem that goes 'Miss Twye was soaping her breasts in the bath / When she heard behind her a meaning laugh / And to her amazement she discovered / A wicked man in the bathroom cupboard'. Ewart worked as an advertising copywriter for many years, along with the Australian Peter Porter, who influenced his return to poetry with *Londoners* (1964). After this re-launch of his career, which Philip Larkin called 'the advent, or perhaps I should say the irruption, of Gavin Ewart', he became prolific, writing many poems with a high degree of technical ingenuity.

In 1948 somebody told me

about Dylan Thomas's behaviour in The Gargoyle,

how he would go round the room on all fours

begging at the tables, like a dog, for a drink.

'Little Dylan wants a little drinkie!'

FROM 'INSULTS TO THE BRAIN', BY

Gavin Ewart

(1916–1995)

A genial and highly sociable man, at least while he was taking anti-psychotic medication, Lowell made the acquaintance of almost every major literary figure of his time, from Ford, Pound and Eliot to Frederick Seidel and Frank Bidart; married three of the novelists he met – Jean Stafford, Elizabeth Hardwick and Caroline Blackwood (the ex-wife of the painter Lucian Freud); and proposed marriage to others – a manic depressive, he often behaved erratically and at times his illness compelled his hospitalisation. One of his compulsions, in his madness, was to re-write all of his work; Randall Jarrell tells him, in one of the sonnets collected in his book *History*, 'You didn't write, you *re*wrote'. Critics saw Lowell's *Life Studies* as the first work of a school of 'Confessional Poets', though it does not confess to anything more than a semi-aristocratic pedigree. Lowell himself disliked the term and rejected it, yet most of the poetry he produced in his later years is a detailed and fascinating record of his life and acquaintances. Perhaps his closest friend was Elizabeth Bishop, who always took care to live as far away from him as possible, leading to a memorable and revealing correspondence that has since been published.

The lobbed ball plops, then dribbles to the cup ...
(a birdie Fordie!) But it nearly killed
the ministers. Lloyd George was holding up
the flag. He gabbled, 'Hop-toad, hop-toad, hop-toad!
Hueffer has used a niblick on the green;
it's filthy art, Sir, filthy art.'

FROM 'FORD MADOX FORD', BY

Robert Lowell

(1917–1977)

All of the poems of the fictional 'Ern Malley' were composed on an idle afternoon during the Second World War by McAuley and Harold Stewart, two army intelligence officers. Their intention was to satirise the increasingly fashionable poetic style that some critics called 'modernism' or 'surrealism', as produced by writers such as Dylan Thomas, David Gascoyne and George Barker. Such writing, McAuley and Stewart believed, could not be distinguished from 'consciously contrived nonsense' by the literary editors who were publishing it. By sending the Malley poems to the little magazine *Angry Penguins*, where they were published as the work of a newly discovered genius, the creators of the poems proved their point. When the hoax was exposed, it caused a furore that was a considerable setback for the career of the magazine's editor, Max Harris, who was also convicted for publishing an 'indecent advertisement'. McAuley went on to become Professor of English at the University of Tasmania, as well as being the foundation editor of *Quadrant*, a magazine supported by the CIA-backed Congress for Cultural Freedom.

In the twenty-fifth year of my age

I find myself to be a dromedary

FROM ERN MALLEY'S 'PETIT TESTAMENT', BY

James McAuley

(1917–1976)

The German word means 'Do not forget me'. Douglas, fighting in the battle of El Alamein, the setting of Kenneth Slessor's 'Beach Burial' (see page 111), found the body of a gunner who had earlier, 'hit my tank with one / like the entry of a demon'. The girl's picture makes him see that 'lover and killer are mingled'. Even as a schoolboy, Douglas was a highly promising poet; at Merton College, Oxford, he was tutored by Edmund Blunden, who had also encouraged Wilfred Owen and Siegfried Sassoon during the First World War. Blunden sent a selection of poems by Douglas to TS Eliot at Faber and Faber; Eliot replied with encouragement but nothing more. Before Douglas could graduate from university, however, war broke out and he enlisted in the army. He survived the explosion of a landmine in Egypt and returned to England briefly to prepare his first book of poetry for another publisher, Editions Poetry London, but was killed in Normandy before it could appear.

Look. Here in the gunpit spoil

the dishonoured picture of his girl

who has put: *Steffi. Vergissmeinnicht*

in a copybook gothic script.

FROM 'VERGISSMEINNICHT', BY

Keith Douglas

(1920–1944)

After the poems she submitted under her own name were belittled and rejected by editors and critics as the work of a mere 'Tasmanian housewife', Harwood devised a series of male pseudonyms and false addresses to accompany her submissions to literary magazines such as *Meanjin* and *The Bulletin*. Soon a critical survey of poetry in Australia praised the work of Francis Geyer and Walter Lehmann, but overlooked Gwen Harwood entirely; as a result, 'Lehmann' sent two acrostic sonnets to *The Bulletin* containing the messages 'So long Bulletin' and 'Fuck all editors'. When scandal erupted over the discovery of the acrostics, their author was referred to in news reports as a 'Tasmanian housewife'. In fact, Harwood was one of the most gifted and technically accomplished poets of her generation, as skilful, in her own way, as her contemporaries Richard Wilbur and Anthony Hecht; her best work even bears comparison with that of Elizabeth Bishop.

The washing machine was chuffing

Ja-PAN Ja-PAN Ja-PAN

as she hustled her husband townwards

and her lonely day began

FROM 'LONG AFTER HEINE', BY

Gwen Harwood

(1920–1995)

During the Second World War, Wilbur served in the US Army in Africa, France and Italy, and several of the poems in his first collection, published in 1947, are an attempt to resolve the chaos of war into some form of order. At every stage of his life, Wilbur's writing was lucid, disciplined and orderly. After the war he taught at Harvard University, and later at other universities, and his poetry has been heaped with praise and honours, including multiple Pulitzer Prizes, but his life was otherwise uneventful compared to those of his contemporaries, which may explain its remarkable length.

The ration stacks are milky domes;

Across the ammunition pile

The snow has climbed in sparkling combs.

You think: beyond the town a mile

Or two, this snowfall fills the eyes

Of soldiers dead a little while.

FROM 'FIRST SNOW IN ALSACE', BY

Richard Wilbur

(1921–2017)

Referring to a WB Yeats poem that appears in almost every modern poetry anthology, Larkin ruefully observed of the work that begins with these famous lines, 'It's becoming my "Lake Isle of Innisfree"'. No poet born in the twentieth century has been quoted more frequently than Larkin, whose direct and unadorned style was seen as an antidote to the ornateness and obscurity of the poets satirised by the 'Ern Malley' hoax, such as Dylan Thomas and George Barker. Larkin's life, too, was considered a rebuke to the romantic or Thomas-like model of the dissipated, irresponsible poet: he appeared to be a lonely bachelor who worked as a librarian in a provincial city, and was thought to be an admirer of Margaret Thatcher. After his death, however, it emerged that he had not married because he preferred to have several different women in his life at once, and that he liked to 'get half-drunk at night', as his poem 'Aubade' puts it. The publication of his letters to one of those women, Monica Jones, revealed a character far more warm, witty and approachable than the misanthropic one presented in his writing, who concludes the poem quoted here with the lines 'Get out as early as you can / And don't have any kids yourself'.

They fuck you up, your mum and dad.

They may not mean to, but they do.

FROM 'THIS BE THE VERSE', BY

Philip Larkin

(1922–1985)

While assigned to the Counter Intelligence Corps of the US Army during the Second World War, Hecht was present at the liberation of the Flossenburg concentration camp, an annex of Buchenwald, in 1945; this first-hand exposure to the operations of the Holocaust meant that for years after he 'would wake shrieking'. Thus each of his books, though witty, elegant, and civilised, and showing a mastery of language and form, is yet 'stalked by occasions of madness, paranoia, hallucination and dream', as his admirer JD McClatchy put it. After the war, Hecht had a long academic career, teaching at Kenyon, Smith and Rochester, as well as being a visiting professor at Harvard while Elizabeth Bishop was teaching there. He was acquainted with all the major poets of his time, including Robert Lowell, Ted Hughes and Sylvia Plath, and the publication of his *Selected Letters* in 2013 revealed that he had corresponded with the Australian writers Chris Wallace-Crabbe, Peter Steele and Alan Frost.

We move now to outside a German wood.

Three men are there commanded to dig a hole

In which the two Jews are ordered to lie down

And be buried alive by the third, who is a Pole.

Not light from the shrine at Weimar beyond the hill

Nor light from heaven appeared. But he did refuse.

A Luger settled back deeply in its glove.

He was ordered to change places with the Jews.

FROM 'MORE LIGHT! MORE LIGHT!', BY

Anthony Hecht

(1923–2004)

he son of a teacher who was also a minor poet, Ginsberg began writing conventional rhymed verse in the manner of the English poets of the sixteenth century. The example of Walt Whitman set him free, and he turned to the long-lined and utterly liberated style that he came to justify with the dictum 'first thought, best thought' (DH Lawrence had a similar theory of poetic composition, saying, 'I have always tried to get an emotion out in its own course, without altering it'). 'Howl', along with Jack Kerouac's *On the Road*, was a founding text for the motley group of writers who came to be known as the Beats, and whose fame eclipsed the literary merit of their work. Ginsberg toured and gave histrionic poetry readings all over the world until he became a part of American popular culture, a figure so recognisable that he was invited to appear in one of Bob Dylan's early promotional film clips.

I saw the best minds of my generation destroyed
by madness, starving hysterical naked,
dragging themselves through the negro streets at dawn
looking for an angry fix

FROM 'HOWL', BY

Allen Ginsberg

(1926–1997)

After an unhappy childhood in Brisbane, Porter moved to London in his early twenties; he lived there in the same rent-controlled flat for the rest of his life. By the late 1960s he had established a reputation and was part of a group of poets known, unimaginatively, as 'The Group'. Porter was an exceptionally charming and erudite companion who came to know everyone in the English poetry scene, including Ted Hughes and Sylvia Plath; in the mid-1970s his wife, Janice, emulated Plath by committing suicide. The lines quoted here clearly refer to Les Murray, who responded to this satirical characterisation with a brilliant prose essay examining the relationship between 'Boetian' and 'Athenian' poets, the former represented by Murray and the latter by Porter. The remarkable success Murray's poetry has enjoyed in Britain was greatly helped, in its early stages, by Porter's generous introductions and contacts.

Like a Taree smallholder splitting logs

And philosophizing on his dangling billies,

The poet mixes hard agrarian instances

With sour sucks to his brother.

FROM 'ON FIRST LOOKING INTO

CHAPMAN'S HESIOD', BY

Peter Porter

(1929–2010)

Born in Barbados, Brathwaite was educated at Pembroke College, Cambridge, before earning a doctorate from the University of Sussex in England. He worked in Ghana for several years then returned to Barbados to take up a position as a history lecturer at the University of the West Indies. In 1993 he became Professor of Comparative Literature at New York University. Brathwaite's poems exploit the unique rhythms and diction of everyday speech in the Caribbean, rhythms that he believed to be at odds with the demands of traditional English verse forms. His poems are full of a vivid sense of place, of the light and the sounds of the islands. At the same time he rages against British colonialism, though his own career appears to have benefited from the spread of English across the world.

But I say it once an' I say it agen:

when things goan' good, you cahn touch

we; but leh murder start

an ol' man, you cahn fine a man to hole up de side ...

FROM 'RITES', BY

Edward Kamau Brathwaite

(1930–)

Born in Yorkshire, Hughes won a scholarship to Pembroke College, Cambridge, where he met an American student called Sylvia Plath; his first collection of poems, *The Hawk in the Rain*, has the dedication 'To Sylvia'. Many of the poems in this book are about war. Though Hughes only joined the air force, as a National Serviceman, after the Second World War, his father fought in the First World War, and had many stories to tell. Hughes married Plath, and they had two children, but it was not a happy marriage, and they had separated by the time Plath committed suicide; Hughes was involved with two other women when this avoidable tragedy took place. More tragedies were to afflict him while his reputation grew. On the death of John Betjeman in 1984, Hughes was appointed Poet Laureate. When he visited Australia in 1976 for Adelaide's Writers Week he proved very popular with the local literary ladies; later, his daughter Frieda moved to Western Australia, where she published her first book of poems.

Farmers in the fields, housewives behind

steamed windows,

Watch the burning aircraft across the blue sky float,

As if a firefly and a spider fought

FROM 'THE CASUALTY', BY

Ted Hughes

(1930–1998)

Unlike his exact contemporary Edward Kamau Brathwaite, Walcott did not believe that the patois of the Caribbean was incompatible with traditional English prosody. Some of his finest poems are in iambic pentameter and tightly rhymed, and in *Omeros* he even re-wrote Homer in a Caribbean setting; yet he was a daring experimental poet, as well, when he needed to be. In 1992 he was awarded the Nobel Prize for Literature for his considerable body of work. Walcott was born on the island of St Lucia, one of twins, soon after the death of his father. He studied art, and became an accomplished watercolourist, before founding the Trinidad Theatre Workshop. In 1977 he moved to America to teach at Boston University, until in 1996 he was sued for sexual harassment by one of his students. In Boston he was encouraged by Robert Lowell and formed a close association with Joseph Brodsky and Seamus Heaney, sharing with them a sense of poetic exile: he wrote of the 'empire' which had made of him a 'colonial upstart', 'It's good that everything's gone, except their language, which is everything'.

these days in bookstores I stand paralyzed

by the rows of shelves along whose wooden branches

the free-verse nightingales are trilling 'Read me!

Read me!'

in various metres of asthmatic pain;

FROM 'NORTH AND SOUTH', BY

Derek Walcott

(1930–2017)

When biographies of those writers regarded (against their volition) as part of the 'Confessional' school of poets are published, the name of Starbuck often comes up. Yet his writing style was cheerful and humorous rather than suicidal. At Harvard University Starbuck studied under Robert Lowell, and among his fellow students were Anne Sexton and Sylvia Plath; he even had an affair with Sexton and was the editor of her first book of poems while he was working for a publisher. Later he became the director of the famous writer's workshop at the University of Iowa before returning to teach at Boston. Starbuck was the most technically ingenious poet of his generation, but his work was sometimes dismissed as mere 'light verse' because he was consistently funny, even when dealing with large-scale and serious subject matter. His ingenuity was hard-won, as he was not a prolific poet. He married three times and fathered five children before he died of Parkinson's disease.

My favorite student lately is the one who wrote about

feeling clumbsy.

I mean if he wanted to say how it feels to be all

thumbs he

Certainly picked the write language to right in in the

first place.

I mean better to clutter a word up like the old

Hearst place

Than to just walk off the job and not give a dam.

Another student gave me a diagragm.

FROM 'THE SPELL AGAINST SPELLING', BY

George Starbuck

(1931–1996)

Before completing her first university degree, at Smith College, Plath experienced her first nervous breakdown and suicide attempt. She then won a Fulbright scholarship to Cambridge University, where she met Ted Hughes and bit him on the face (perhaps this was why she said 'I eat men like air'). Soon afterwards she married Hughes. The marriage was not a success, even though it produced two children and a considerable body of poetry from both partners, as well as Plath's novel *The Bell Jar*. Plath and Hughes were living separately by the time of her suicide, which has been attributed to various causes, including her rejection by two other men and an exceptionally cold winter. To feminists, Ted Hughes was to blame for her death, even though her reputation derived in large part from his editing and promotion of *Ariel*, her last and most 'confessional' book, which was found unpublished after she had gassed herself, leaving her children safe upstairs.

Out of the ash

I rise with my red hair

And I eat men like air.

FROM 'LADY LAZARUS', BY

Sylvia Plath

(1932–1963)

n 1960, Seidel interviewed Robert Lowell for *The Paris Review*. During 2017, thirteen new poems by Seidel appeared in the same journal, after the publication of his latest collection, *Widening Income Inequality*, in 2016. His literary energy, in his eighties, is astonishing, as are the poems themselves: they are the poems of a man who has no fear of received opinions, resisting contemporary ideas of political convention and old-fashioned decency alike with striking, and highly amusing, candour. The voice of Seidel's poetry is all his own, but his technique recalls somewhat the method of Ogden Nash, with lines of irregular and unpredictable length end-stopped by at times inventive rhymes. Those lines are alternately outrageously over-sexed, or boastful about his family wealth ('I'm from the Seidel Coal and Coke Company and the Mississippi'), or obsessed with fast cars and motorbikes; they are as compelling as they are shocking.

My oh my. How times have changed.

But the fanatics have gotten even more deranged.

Seventy-five years after Hitler toured charming,

   cheering Paris, Parisians say

They won't give in to terrorist tyranny, and yesterday

Two million people marched arm in arm, hand in hand,

After the latest murderous horror

FROM 'FRANCE NOW', BY

Frederick Seidel

(1936–)

I n the early 1990s, the critic Blake Morrison observed of Murray that he was by then 'one of the finest poets writing in English, one of a superleague that includes Seamus Heaney, Derek Walcott and Joseph Brodsky'. Heaney, Walcott and Brodsky each went on to be awarded the Nobel Prize for Literature, but Murray did not; on the other hand, Murray is still alive, while the other three have died. Brodsky described Murray as 'the one by whom the language lives', referring to the lines Auden excised from his poem about WB Yeats (see page 117). It is not enough to see Murray as Australia's greatest poet; he is the country's greatest writer in any genre. The lines quoted here intentionally echo the closing lines of 'Fern Hill', by Dylan Thomas, as the poem is set in Wales. Its subject is the only vice Murray has been guilty of, which is to say eating, rather than the drinking, drug-taking and womanising pursued by many other poets. For over thirty years he has been Literary Editor of *Quadrant*.

I signed my plate in the end with a licked knife

and fork

and green-and-gold spotted, I sang for my pains

like the free

before I passed out among all the stars of Cilfynydd.

FROM 'VINDALOO IN MERTHYR TYDFIL', BY

Les Murray

(1938–)

The opening lines of the first poem in the first book Heaney published in some ways summarise all of the words that were to follow. The clusters of consonants, the internal rhymes, the abrupt monosyllables, the iambic metre – all anticipate the literary techniques that would serve Heaney so well that he would, in 1995, receive the Nobel Prize for Literature. At the same time the content of these lines reflects two subjects that recur throughout his work: the pen represents his interest in the process of writing itself, while the gun alludes to the Troubles in Northern Ireland, a conflict in which Heaney was always careful not to be seen taking sides, though its presence would act as a backdrop for many of his best poems. After growing up on a farm, Heaney attended Queen's University at Belfast, and for most of his working life he taught at universities around the world, including Queen's, Harvard and Oxford, where he was elected Professor of Poetry.

Between my finger and my thumb

The squat pen rests; snug as a gun.

FROM 'DIGGING', BY

Seamus Heaney

(1939–2013)

James was a student at Sydney University at the same time as Les Murray, but like Peter Porter he soon moved to England and did not come back. After further study at Cambridge, he found a position as a television critic, and this led to him becoming a television personality in his own right. Yet even while he lived in the spotlight of international celebrity, he continued to see himself as a poet, writing mock epics in Pope-like couplets and publishing verse diaries and verse letters addressed to other international celebrities. When he retired from television he turned to poetry as never before, turning out book-length collections at a rate no other poet so craft-obsessed has matched. As a poet, James is highly literary, and many of his poems, like the one quoted here, are as much works of literary criticism as they are creative outpourings. In 2011 he announced his imminent death from cancer, but his demise has not yet arrived, and in the six years since that announcement he has published more than half a dozen books, including poetry, prose and an admired translation of Dante's entire *Divine Comedy*.

His stunning first lines burst out of the page
Like a man thrown through a windscreen.
   His flat drawl
Was acrid with the spirit of the age –
The spy's last cigarette, the hungry sprawl
Of Hornby clockwork train sets

FROM 'WHAT HAPPENED TO AUDEN', BY

Clive James

(1939–)

Though his reputation has been overshadowed by that of his Nobel Prize–winning contemporary Seamus Heaney, Mahon is if anything the more complete poet of the two. His writing has always been admired for its technical skill, and it is at times as witty as Peter Porter's, while dealing with serious subject matter. His poems often move from a commonplace local setting (as in his famous poem 'A Disused Shed in Co. Wexford') to the cosmic and epic. Though he gained a degree from Trinity College, Dublin, he did not become an academic, instead earning a living as a freelance writer, editor and BBC scriptwriter for many years, and working for such journals as *The Listener*, *New Statesman* and *Vogue*.

The wind that blows these words to you

bangs nightly off the black-and-blue

Atlantic, hammering in its haste

dark doors of the declining west

FROM 'BEYOND HOWTH HEAD', BY

Derek Mahon

(1941–)

n late middle age, Williams has been treated for kidney failure, and the poems in the sequence entitled 'From the Dialysis Ward' are one fortunate result — fortunate, that is, for his readers. In praising the 'ease of manner and dandyishness' of Williams as a poet, Michael Hofmann went on to add 'he is utterly English'. This may be because his mother was an Australian actress, Margaret Vyner, who had moved to England in the 1930s in the hope of meeting the actor Hugh Williams. Their son Simon Williams became an actor as well, while Hugo, who left school at the age of seventeen and did not go to university, has worked as a journalist and travel writer to support his poetry-writing habit.

Ray Blighter appears in the doorway

of the dialysis ward

in all his ruined finery –

waistcoat, buttonhole, blazer,

eyebrows dashed in with mascara –

and pauses for a moment to ensure

all eyes are upon him.

'MY NAME IS BOND,' he shouts

to the assembled company,

'JAMES FUCKING BOND.'

FROM 'RAY'S WAY', BY

Hugo Williams

(1942–)

Dunn was born in Renfrewshire in Scotland and studied librarianship. One of his first jobs was at the University of Hull, where the head librarian was Philip Larkin. He and Larkin became close, but Dunn's early poetry is sprightly and satirical, showing little sign of Larkin's influence, even though most of the poems in his first collection, *Terry Street*, are set in the slums of Hull. The tone of Dunn's poetry was understandably altered by the death of his first wife, Lesley, when she was only thirty-seven. That event was memorialised in his powerful collection *Elegies*, where he describes how 'She sat up on her pillows, receiving guests. / I brought them tea or sherry like a butler / Up and down the thirteen steps from my pantry.' He has nevertheless continued to be a prolific poet, polished in technique and always lucid and readable, despite his heartbreaking loss.

Cricket players have the manners of ghosts,

Wandering in white on the tended ground.

They go in now, walking in twos and threes.

This sight is worth a week of evenings.

FROM 'CLOSE OF PLAY', BY

Douglas Dunn

(1942–)

The oldest son in a family of exceptional sportsmen – one brother was New Zealand's finest batsman of his time, while the youngest was a successful golfer – Turner ranks as highly as a poet as his brothers do as game-players. In addition to his work as poet, editor, ghost-writer and memoirist, Turner himself has been a sportsman of remarkable versatility, playing first-class cricket for Otago, international field hockey for New Zealand, cycling competitively well into his fifties, and earning a handsome income as a professional golf caddy. His poetry is versatile also, and includes both haiku-like image-based poems like this one, and more expansive pieces rich with typically laconic New Zealand humour.

A curdle of sheep wobbles by

leaving freckles

and liver spots

all over the road.

'MOVING STOCK', BY

Brian Turner

(1944–)

The success of Raine's second book, *A Martian Sends a Postcard Home*, was such that critics identified him as the leader of a new literary movement, known as the Metaphor Men or the Martian School. The school comprised, among others, Raine himself, Christopher Reid and the novelist Martin Amis. The 'Martian' style relied on strikingly original metaphors relayed in the coolly neutral tone of an alien scientist seeing the everyday objects of our world for the first time. Like most fashions, the Martian School had its time (in the early 1980s) and then faded from view, but Raine has continued to produce strong, metaphor-rich poetry, as well as being a formidable critic for journals such as *The Spectator* and the *TLS*. He has also been a university lecturer, and for ten years was poetry editor at Faber and Faber, the position once held by TS Eliot.

Wasps with Donald McGill bathing suits

were learning to swim in my cider glass.

A wagtail nervously patted the crease

and noted the way the field was placed,

while the cat crouched low for a catch

FROM 'FACTS OF LIFE', BY

Craig Raine

(1944–)

By the time Craig Raine came to publish his first book of poems, Gray was already the author of two major collections, the second of them endorsed by the Nobel Prize winner Patrick White. Yet Gray could be seen as Australia's representative of the Martian School, except that for all the brilliance of the imagery in his poems he tends to favour simile over metaphor, and instead of the unemotional 'alien' tone of the 'Martian' poets his writing is suffused with unstated but unmistakable feeling. Gray left school early and did not attend university; instead, he worked in advertising for a time, alongside the son of Dylan Thomas, before he was employed in a Paddington bookshop owned by William de Winton, the great-grandson of Lady Gregory, patron of WB Yeats.

three or four geese let loose and rushing

with their heads beating sideways like metronomes,

towards a dam where the mountain-top hung;

and when they entered the water, the mountain's

image came apart

suddenly, the way a cabbage falls into coleslaw.

FROM 'CURRICULUM VITAE', BY

Robert Gray

(1945–)

Like Clive James, Cope is one of those poets whose writing emerges largely from their reading: her subject is often the process of writing or the literary world, while some of her most amusing poems are parodies of other well-known poets, including a version of TS Eliot's 'The Waste Land' reduced to a series of limericks. The title of her best-selling first collection of poetry, *Making Cocoa for Kingsley Amis*, is an example of this tendency. Cope worked as a primary school teacher before the success of her first book enabled her to become a freelance writer; she then became a television critic, like Clive James, for *The Spectator*, and she has also been a wise and witty book reviewer.

I think I am in love with A.E. Housman,

Which puts me in a worse than usual fix.

No woman ever stood a chance with Housman

And he's been dead since 1936.

'ANOTHER UNFORTUNATE CHOICE', BY

Wendy Cope

(1945–)

Hadas grew up in New York City and studied at Radcliffe College before moving to Greece for four years. She completed a doctorate at Princeton University after her return, and has been teaching in the English Department of Rutgers University in New Jersey for many years. She was married to the composer George Edwards, who died in 2011. Her reputation, which has earned her several major awards and fellowships, rests not only on the quality of her poetry, which is notably skilful and witty, but also on her achievements as a translator.

The same sea, says Elizabeth Bishop.

Over and over, the same, the same.

I disagree, says Heraclitus.

You can't step into it again

(he means the river). Both are right,

and both are wrong.

FROM 'NEUROLOGY FLOOR', BY

Rachel Hadas

(1948–)

While studying at Magdalen College in Oxford, Fenton won the Newdigate Prize for Poetry; he then worked as a journalist and war correspondent before returning to Oxford as Professor of Poetry in the late 1990s. His literary reputation rests on a quite slim body of work, as much of his creative energy has been expended on more profitable endeavours, including not only political journalism, travel writing, book reviews and theatre criticism, but also his contribution to the musical adaptation of Victor Hugo's *Les Miserables*, for which he has earned royalty payments beyond the normal expectations of a poet. In recent years he has lived in New York with the writer and novelist Daryl Pinckney, and been frequently published in *The New York Review of Books*.

Death is the envy of the hicks,

The last crap shot, the final fix,

It is the burning of the ricks.

   Lovelier than sex, it

Beckons us home across the Styx

   And we must exit.

FROM 'LETTER TO JOHN FULLER', BY

James Fenton

(1949–)

Born in California, Gioia attended Stanford University before completing a master's degree at Harvard, where he studied under Elizabeth Bishop. He then returned to Stanford and gained a business degree, and went on to work for the General Foods company (maker of Jell-O, among other products), becoming Vice-President of Marketing while writing poetry and criticism at night. The success of his essay 'Can Poetry Matter?', first published in *The Atlantic* in 1991, encouraged him to resign to concentrate on his writing career. He has since become a professor of poetry at the University of Southern California, and for six years he was the chairman of the National Endowment for the Arts, where his business experience proved most valuable.

Let me confess. I'm sick of these sestinas
written by youngsters in poetry workshops
for the delectation of their fellow students,
and then published in little magazines
that no one reads, not even the contributors
who at least in this omission show some taste.

FROM 'MY CONFESSIONAL SESTINA', BY

Dana Gioia

(1950–)

Like Randall Jarrell, Logan has been as highly regarded for his criticism as for his poetry; unlike Jarrell, he has been prolific in both capacities, and he has not died young. For many years he has divided his time between teaching positions at the University of Florida and at Cambridge University in England; the settings of his poems are similarly divided. To some he is best known as the poetry critic for *The New Criterion*, a magazine that could be considered the successor to *Encounter*, though it lacks the sponsorship of the CIA, where his reviews are entertaining in their precise and logical approach to the vagueness and illogicality of many poets' pretensions. His one blind spot appears to be the poetry of Les Murray; he seems unable to imagine Murray's words pronounced in an Australian accent.

Hull was a rainy country. The damp of suits

slumped on their wooden hangers understairs,

the wet umbrellas dying in the hall.

The ink-stained carpet. The sodden shoes. The hats.

FROM 'BRIEF LIVES – I. LARKIN', BY

William Logan

(1950–)

Leithauser could be seen as a successor to Marianne Moore, writing in complex syllabic stanzas with rhymes in unusual positions (in the passage quoted, a rhyming word is hidden in the middle of a line), and like Moore his subject is often a fastidiously detailed study of some such creature as a frog, toad or turtle. Leithauser was born in Detroit and graduated from Harvard Law School; for several years he lived in Japan as a fellow at the Kyoto Comparative Law Center. Like Robert Browning and Ted Hughes he married a fellow poet, Mary Jo Salter; the marriage, like that of Hughes, ended in divorce. For most of his career, he has worked as a university teacher of English.

Binoculars I'd meant for birds

catch instead, and place an arm's length away

a frog

compactly perched on a log that lies

half in, half out of the river.

FROM 'BETWEEN LEAPS', BY

Brad Leithauser

(1953–)

Like many of the writers who have visited Australia, from DH Lawrence onwards, Salter was unable to resist the oddity of the kangaroo; she also wrote a powerful poem based on Charles Sturt's exploration of the inland after her attendance at the Mildura Writers Festival in 1997. Salter was born in Michigan, and completed a degree at Harvard University, where she studied under Elizabeth Bishop, before undertaking a higher degree at Cambridge University. She has taught in various universities for many years and is one of the editors of *The Norton Anthology of Poetry*.

Like flustered actors
who don't know what to do
with their hands, they're hanging
around in awkward clusters,
paws dangling, ears pricked for a cue.

FROM 'KANGAROO', BY

Mary Jo Salter

(1954–)

For many writers born after the Second World War, illness has become their battleground, and Hodgins is the Wilfred Owen of the hospital ward. Aged only twenty-four, he was diagnosed with leukemia and told he had just three years to live; he survived for twelve, and in that time produced a body of work any writer with a normal life span would have been proud of. Despite his illness he travelled widely, and he even had his poetry published in *The New Yorker*; his subject matter varies from vivid memories of his rural upbringing, where his eye for detail is as clear as that of Les Murray, to observations of his travel in Europe, where his sophistication equals that of Peter Porter. Always, though, he returns to the death sentence that hangs over him. After his death the Mildura Writers Festival was established in his honour.

But since I got the only part

in cancer's scripted dialogue

I've heard those birds a million times

and seen the sun come up a lot.

I've been rehearsing death each night,

and still I haven't got it right.

FROM 'THE BIRDS', BY

Philip Hodgins

(1959–1995)

Stallings (the initials stand for Alicia Elsbeth) studied classics at the University of Georgia, and then at Oxford University. Her first collection of poetry won the Richard Wilbur Award in 1999, and in the same year she moved to Athens in Greece, where her husband is the editor of *The Athens News*. As a poet, she is known for her skill in handling traditional verse forms, a skill which can also be seen in her well-regarded work as a translator, and which has earned her many prizes and fellowships.

In Anhedonia we take

Our bitters with hypnotic waters.

The dawn's always about to break

But never does. We dream of daughters.

FROM 'PERSEPHONE TO PSYCHE', BY

AE Stallings

(1968–)

The opening lines of Dante's *Inferno* are referred to, or translated, here, while the form used echoes that of Louis Mac-Neice's *Autumn Journal*. Quinn, like MacNeice, is an Irish poet who does not live in Ireland. He gained a doctorate from Trinity College, Dublin, then moved to the Czech Republic to teach at the Charles University in Prague; as a result, his poems have an international sophistication even when they return to the Ireland of his upbringing. Quinn was one of the founding editors of the literary journal *Metre*, in which formalism and cosmopolitanism were encouraged. As a poet, he is as much at home in regular rhyme and metre as he is in free verse and even prose poems, and his use of language is always direct and often witty, despite being haunted, at times, by the violence of our age.

Then in the middle of it all

I woke to find myself in a deep forest,

The light dismal,

Moon-glow seeping downward through the trees,

and frost

Enamelling the ground.

FROM 'EPIC FRAGMENT', BY

Justin Quinn

(1968–)

The allusion is to Robert Frost's 'Nothing Gold Can Stay'. Hannah appeared to be a successor to Wendy Cope when she burst onto the poetry scene in her twenties, producing five books in quick succession that were full of witty responses to other poets and amusing observations of contemporary society, all framed in highly polished and regular traditional verse forms. She then reversed the literary trajectory followed by Thomas Hardy by going from poetry to fiction and becoming a best-selling crime novelist whose books have been adapted for television, as well as impersonating the long-dead Agatha Christie by devising new adventures for Christie's character Hercule Poirot. She has also published translations of children's verse books.

You buy your trainers new.

They cost a bob or two.

At first they're clean and white,

The laces thick and tight.

Then they must touch the ground –

(You have to walk around).

You learn to your dismay

Trainers all turn grey.

'TRAINERS ALL TURN GREY', BY

Sophie Hannah

(1971–)

On one hand, Smith has written image-based poems that invite comparison with the work of Craig Raine and Robert Gray; on the other, she is the author of witty social commentary reminiscent of Wendy Cope and Sophie Hannah. Yet this is only the beginning of her versatility as a poet, one who is equally at home with traditional verse forms and with every kind of experimentation. Smith lives in Canberra and has worked as a lawyer; she is also the mother of two young children. In 2014 she was awarded the Australian Prime Minister's Literary Award for Poetry.

just off the headland

the seaweed-furred rocks

keep drawing over themselves

– and casting off again –

thick veils of tumbled glistening lace

FROM 'BONDI SKETCHES', BY

Melinda Smith

(1971–)

Credits

Published in 2018 by Hardie Grant Books,
an imprint of Hardie Grant Publishing

Hardie Grant Books (Melbourne)
Building 1, 658 Church Street
Richmond, Victoria 3121

Hardie Grant Books (London)
5th & 6th Floors
52–54 Southwark Street
London SE1 1UN

hardiegrantbooks.com

A Cataloguing-in-Publication entry is available from the catalogue of the
National Library of Australia at www.nla.gov.au

Lasting Lines: 100 poems and poets you should know
ISBN 978 1 74379 424 1

Cover, text design and typesetting by Peter Long
Printed in China by 1010 Printing International Limited

Every effort has been made to incorporate correct information and to attribute
copyright. The publishers regret any errors and omissions and invite readers to
contribute up-to-date or additional relevant information to Hardie Grant Books.